# RAGGIN'

# RAGGIN'

## A Story about Scott Joplin

by Barbara Mitchell

illustrations by Hetty Mitchell

A Carolrhoda Creative Minds Book

Carolrhoda Books, Inc./Minneapolis

*To Hal Schiff, for giving me music*

*This book is available in two editions:*
Library binding by Carolrhoda Books, Inc.
Soft cover by First Avenue Editions
c/o The Lerner Group
241 First Avenue North
Minneapolis, MN 55401

LIBRARY OF CONGRESS CATALOGING-IN-PUBLICATION DATA

Mitchell, Barbara, 1941-
    Raggin': a story about Scott Joplin.

    (A Carolrhoda creative minds book)
    Summary: The life story of the black Texan who became a popular
composer and sought to elevate ragtime to the level of classical music,
only to have his talents fully recognized after his death.
    1. Joplin, Scott, 1868-1917—Juvenile literature.
2. Composers—United States—Biography—Juvenile literature.
[1. Joplin, Scott, 1868-1917. 2. Composers. 3. Afro-Americans—
Biography] I. Mitchell, Hetty, ill. II. Title. III. Series.
ML3930.J66M57    1987        780'.92'4[B] [92]        87-9310
ISBN 0-87614-310-9 (lib. bdg.)
ISBN 0-87614-589-6 (pbk.)

Manufactured in the United States of America
6   7   8   9   10   11   -   P/MA   -   00   99   98   97   96   95

# Table of Contents

# AUTHOR'S NOTE

Tracking down the story of this talented composer involved much detective work. As is the case with so many black Americans, very few records were kept of events in the lives of black artists in the early 1900s. I would like to thank author James Haskins for his book *Scott Joplin: The Man Who Made Ragtime* (Garden City, NY, 1978). Mr. Haskins and coresearcher Kathleen Benson spent seven years studying the life of Scott Joplin.

Another account that was a great help to me was *They All Played Ragtime* by Rudi Blesh and Harriet Janis (New York, 1971). This title includes recollections of the composer by those who knew Joplin or his family and friends.

A thank you is due also to Jim and Barbara Vitale, organizers of the annual ragtime festival and contest held at Mill Bridge Village in Strasburg, Pennsylvania, each summer. Their program enabled me to observe, firsthand, a raggers' competition. Judge Ed Pruitt explained the intricacies of ragtime contest performing to me, and he and his wife, Jeanne, kindly posed in their period costumes for the benefit of the artist.

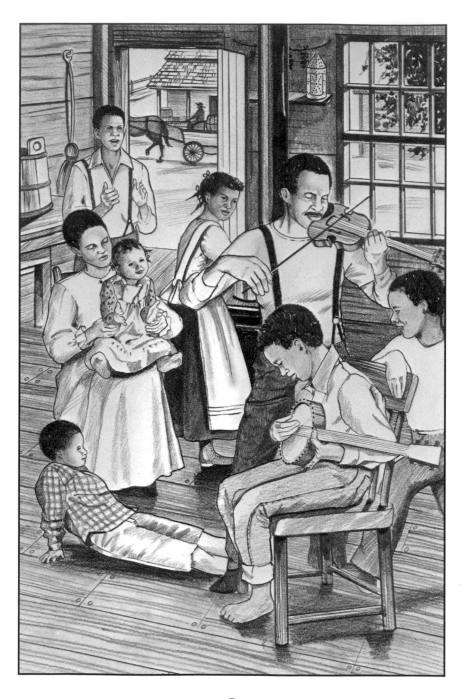

# Chapter One

The red Texas sun had gone down. A breeze made its way into the little frame house on Pine Street. The long, hot working day was over.

"Play me a happy tune, Scott," Florence Joplin said. "Music blows my cares away."

Twelve-year-old Scott took up his mother's old banjo and picked one of her favorite songs. All the Joplins loved music, but Scott's abilities outshone the rest. He was able to remember songs well and played his mother's favorites by ear.

Florence Joplin put up her tired feet and began to sing along. Ten-year-old Osie, stirring a pot of stewed okra and tomatoes, started to hum. Monroe, almost a man now, joined in with his strong, deep voice. Scott's little brothers, Robert and Willie, and even his baby sister, Myrtle, started to clap. Papa kicked off his dirt-caked railroader's boots and took up his violin. The Texarkana street was soon full of the sounds of the music-making Joplins on this fall evening in 1880.

Texarkana was an unusual town. Half of it was in Texas, and the other half was across the state border in Arkansas. Jiles and Florence Joplin and their family lived on the Texas side in the black section of town.

There was nothing fancy about the black neighborhood. Chickens scratched and pigs rooted in the sandy yards. Most of the houses were too small for the families that lived in them. No one had come right out and said, "Because you are black, you must live here," but better houses in other neighborhoods of this fast-growing railroad town were priced higher than any black family could afford. Being black in the years following the Civil War meant being poor.

Most of the black families who had drifted over into Texas from the plantations of the Deep South worked as sharecroppers. They farmed white men's land in return for barely enough money to support themselves and their families. Papa had been able to find work with the Iron Mountain and Southern Railroad. He spent his days repairing track with an ax and pick. Mama's days were filled with washing, ironing, and housecleaning for white families. It was up to Osie to keep the Joplin household going. Just last spring, Osie had nursed four-year-old Willie and newborn Myrtle through the measles. Then when Osie came down with the red rash, too, Scott and nine-year-old Robert had taken over.

It was not a happy time, that spring of 1880. Besides the sickness, Mama and Papa were always arguing. The children were not quite sure why. Scott worried that it was over him. Mama had allowed him to take piano lessons with Mag Washington over on Laurel Street. Mag Washington was a teacher in the school for black children that Scott attended. She enjoyed giving piano lessons to the children in her classes who showed special musical ability. None of her students could afford to have a piano at home.

Papa disapproved of the piano lessons. Scott's love of music was growing stronger every day, and Jiles Joplin feared that his son would come to love music so much that he would want to become a professional musician. Making a living in music was hard, next to impossible, for a black musician. Jiles was sure that his wife was carrying this music business too far.

Mama insisted, though. Scott had a gift, his teacher said, and Florence Joplin agreed. Scott arrived at each weekly lesson bearing a freshly baked pan of cornbread or a sack of black-eyed peas as payment. Florence also began taking Scott with her whenever she cleaned for the Cook family. Mrs. Cook had a piano in her parlor. While Mama scrubbed and polished, Scott practiced the music from his lessons and played the sheet music by Stephen Foster and John Philip Sousa that was always piled on top of the beautiful instrument.

Whatever the cause, the arguing between Papa and Mama did not let up; when the snow came, Papa moved out. It was odd, thought Scott, who had no sure idea of why Papa had left. Music had always united the Joplin family. Could it be music that was now pulling them apart? The only thing he knew for sure was that music brought joy and comfort to his own life. He could *never* give it up.

Soon after Papa left, Scott's brother Monroe left home to take a job as a cook in another town. Florence Joplin moved the rest of her five children over to the Arkansas side of town where rent was cheaper. She took a new job as caretaker of Mount Zion, the town's only black church.

The children missed their friends and their old house. They missed Papa and his violin. Jiles Joplin was a fine fiddler. He had begun playing as a very young boy in an east Texas plantation orchestra. Young Jiles had learned the tunes of the popular European-style dances as he played his violin at the plantation house. Scott missed hearing these dance tunes, but most of all he missed hearing the lively, rhythmic African melodies Papa had learned in the slave quarter.

Although the family missed Papa and his violin, they did not stop playing their own music. One day a secondhand piano arrived at the house. Mama had managed to save enough of her earnings to buy it especially for Scott. Mama thought of the purchase as a necessity. She believed that music could help people rejoice in the pleasures of life as well as help comfort them during hard times.

Music and their life at church gave the Joplin family strength. Scott was 13 now and, with Papa and Monroe gone, the man of the family. It was his place to join in the ring shout at each church service.

Scott stood with the other men of the church as they formed a circle to begin the ring shout.

The best shouter moved into the middle and began a low chant. Women and children stood quietly by—but not for long. The fervent chant-prayer steadily grew stronger and stronger. Scott began to chant with the other men and was swept along with the rhythm as more and more voices joined in. Hands began to clap, feet began to stomp, and soon the small church throbbed with the rhythm of the movement and the chant.

When the perspiring shouters were too tired to go on, somebody began to sing a quiet spiritual. Scott was filled with a deep sadness as the room echoed with the mournful melodies that were sung in slave quarters years ago. The rhythm and emotion of the shout were just what his soul craved.

Scott's weekdays were filled with music, too. He had begun to study with Mr. J.C. Johnson. Johnson was known as "Professor" around town. He played and taught only classical music. Scott saved up the nickels and dimes he earned carrying water to thirsty railroad workers so he could buy music books that his teacher recommended. He wanted to learn about every kind of music there was.

When Scott was 16, he, his brother Will, and two neighborhood boys formed a singing group that performed at parties and dances around town. By the time he was 20, the desire to be a professional musician had completely taken hold of him, just as Papa had predicted. Most of Scott's friends were taking jobs with the local railroad, but Scott had ideas that would take him far from home. There were jobs in music to be had on the boats that sailed America's mightiest river, the Mississippi, and Scott was determined to get one.

# Chapter Two

White steamboats with bright red paddlewheels churned the Mississippi River's muddy waters. Unlike the flat barges that traveled up and down the river, the paddlewheelers did not carry cargo. Instead, they carried passengers bound for big cities such as St. Louis and New Orleans. A showy riverboat usually had a calliope on board. The tall, golden steam whistles of a calliope were played by a mechanical keyboard, and this musical wonder kept passengers fascinated by the hour. A luxury riverboat often traveled the river with a live band as well as a calliope aboard for entertainment.

The owners of the smaller steamboats could afford neither live bands nor calliopes. They could hire only a single banjo player, or perhaps a pianist, to entertain the passengers. It was on one of these vessels that Scott found a job.

The crowd that formed around the riverboat piano that Joplin played was made up of loud, rough boatmen and travelers who often knew and cared little about music. Scott found himself all but ignored or, worse yet, struggling to be heard above a hubbub of loud talk and laughter. Discouraging as his audience was, Scott kept playing. It was a start, an opening into the world of music that he so wanted to enter.

When a riverboat docked at a town along the way, the people of the town would come running to meet it. The boat's entertainers would usually put on a show for the townspeople with the hope of earning a few coins. Often the musicians would leave the ship to try their luck at jobs in the area playing for fairs, dances, traveling shows, and in saloons. When playing opportunities were exhausted, the musicians would board another boat or hop a train to the next river town. This was how Scott Joplin spent his first several years away from home.

Toward the turn of the century, a new kind of popular music began to take its place alongside the marches and the quiet sentimental songs Scott had played on the Cook's parlor piano back home. The new music was called *ragtime*.

Ragtime was "dancin' music"—played on a piano. With the left hand, the pianist beat out a strong, stomping rhythm, while the right hand added a snappy melody, created by *syncopation.* Syncopation is simply moving the accent from a strong beat to a weaker one. To most white people of the 1880s and 1890s, this piano music sounded unusual, to say the least. They were used to a quieter, tamer style of music. Ragtime was wild!

Ragtime may have seemed wild to white listeners, but to Scott Joplin and many other black listeners it was perfectly natural. Its lively rhythm had grown out of the church shouts and old African dances such as the struts and hops that Jiles Joplin had played on his fiddle. One of these dances, known as the cakewalk, was especially popular in black communities. Strutting, prancing, and promenading were all part of this fascinating dance performed for a prize, which was usually an elaborately decorated cake that the winners would share with the other dancers. Joplin's familiarity with the cakewalk and other roots of ragtime allowed him to quickly and easily make this exciting new music a part of his piano style.

Around 1890, Scott Joplin spent some time in St. Louis, Missouri. St. Louis was a bustling port.

It was packed with saloons where the riverboat men enjoyed gambling their earnings. The saloons were where the "raggers" gathered, too, especially at "Honest John" Turpin's. Turpin's Silver Dollar Saloon had become the place to find a job playing ragtime. The ragtime pianists showed off their skills, hoping their audience of traveling rivermen would recommend them for jobs in other towns.

The Silver Dollar's customers soon found themselves leaving the gambling tables for the piano when Scott played. Nobody played ragtime like Joplin! He had developed a style so much his own that passersby could say, "Listen! Joplin is playing." Word spread quickly throughout St. Louis, and before long Scott was in demand in other Missouri towns such as Hannibal and Sedalia. People from as far away as Louisville, Kentucky, and Cincinnati, Ohio, were coming to hear him play.

Scott earned enough money to live on by playing in saloons all over the Midwest. Wandering from job to job, however, was not what the serious young musician wanted to do with his life. What Scott really wanted was to settle down and be a composer.

Becoming a composer was not easy, however,

especially for a black musician. In those years not so far past slavery, a black pianist could not even perform in a concert hall, let alone write music for it. Besides, music publishers did not think of ragtime as concert music, so they were afraid to put their money into it. And there was yet another problem—nobody had quite figured out how to write ragtime down. Raggers simply sat at barroom pianos and played. How on earth could one get this syncopated, "ragged" music down on paper? Publishers weren't sure it was possible.

There were publishers and listeners, too, who were not interested in working out these problems because they considered any music that had grown out of the slave tradition to be insignificant. Scott, however, believed that ragtime deserved to be taken seriously. Scott Joplin had a gentle spirit, but he was also a man of great determination. So he kept traveling and playing, gathering more and more followers on his way.

In 1893, Scott joined hundreds of other people on their way to Chicago for the Chicago World's Fair. Also known as the World's Columbian Exposition, the fair was created to honor Columbus's discovery of North America. The fair's offerings were said to be so spectacular that the organizers had ended up having to set the opening back a year. Joplin and other traveling raggers believed the world event would be a fine place to show off their playing skills.

Much to their dismay, however, the raggers found that they were not welcome to perform inside the fairgrounds. The musical offerings had all been prearranged. They included concert bands, vocalists, and minstrel shows—but no ragtime. Being excluded from performing inside the fairgrounds did not stop the uninvited raggers from enjoying one another's company and comparing playing skills, though. Word soon got around that the place to hear ragtime music was in the Chicago night clubs where the raggers were meeting and playing for growing crowds of listeners.

Among the visiting raggers was a man named Otis Saunders. Saunders, a pianist from Springfield, Missouri, was himself a Joplin fan. When he and Scott met, Scott told him of his dream to get his work published. "Such fine compositions *should* be written down," Saunders insisted.

There was opportunity for black musicians in the concert world now, Saunders informed his new friend. He took Scott to a performance on the fairgrounds to prove his point. Onstage was the Creole Show, which featured a group of black musicians. The show had a minstrel format. Scott had seen minstrels before; the minstrel shows had come to every riverboat town he'd been in. The shows that Scott had seen were performed by white men whose faces had been made up to look black. These shows, written by white composers, consisted of songs and skits that made southern plantation life sound wonderful. In between songs, there were skits and jokes that poked fun at the plight of the slaves.

The Creole Show was a minstrel show with a difference. There were no degrading jokes, the performers were black, and the music Scott and Otis heard had been drawn from *authentic* African tunes. Scott recognized the sound at once. He had grown up with it. The Creole Show marked a turning point for Scott Joplin. He began to really believe that his own music could be published.

Scott Joplin and Otis Saunders became good friends. When they left the fair, they went on to St. Louis together. Saunders became Scott's unofficial manager, bringing more and more listeners to hear Joplin's music wherever Scott played.

The new gathering spot for raggers in St. Louis was the Rosebud Café. The Rosebud had been opened recently by "Honest John" Turpin's son Tom, who was himself a ragger.

St. Louis was not the only Missouri town where raggers were gathering. Sedalia, Missouri, was also attracting raggers in great numbers. About 190 miles west of St. Louis, this junction of seven railroads was a meeting place for music lovers from well beyond the local area. For Scott, there was yet another reason to go to Sedalia—on the outskirts of the town was a college for black students called Smith College. Scott had long wanted to study musical composition in order to advance his music-writing skills. But to go to college? It seemed a farfetched idea to the young man who had come from little Texarkana. Otis Saunders continued to encourage Scott. "You *must* take classes at Smith," Saunders said. Scott was soon taking courses in music composition at Smith College.

Most publishers at this time were still afraid that this lively music, once written down, would lose its unique ragged quality. Some publishers, though, began taking chances, and a rag written by a white composer in New York was published in

1897. It was followed later that same year by the first publication of a black composer's rag— "Harlem Rag," written by Scott's friend Tom Turpin.

Ragtime and the still-popular cakewalk were now beginning to sweep the entire nation. No longer was this entertainment limited to black audiences in the Midwest. Now Americans everywhere joined the fun, as did dancers in the elegant drawing rooms of faraway Paris.

With the popularity of ragtime music on the rise, Scott decided it was time to make his dream of becoming a composer come true.

# Chapter Three

A new night club was opening in Sedalia in 1898, and Otis Saunders happened to know the owners. "I know a way to make the Maple Leaf Club an instant success," he told Will and Walker Williams.

Walker raised an eyebrow. "An instant success?"

Saunders nodded. "Hire Scott Joplin as your resident pianist," he said.

Walker looked at his partner, then back at Otis. "I believe you have something there, Saunders," he said. "Tell Joplin the job is his."

Otis told Scott the happy news. Scott was pleased. As resident pianist, he would no longer have to wander about looking for work, which would leave him plenty of time for composing.

The Maple Leaf Club was on Sedalia's Main Street. Unlike the many little saloons in the lower sections of towns where Scott had played as a traveling pianist, the Maple Leaf Club attracted the town's leading citizens. The Maple Leaf had style. Gas lamps hung over the tables and the tall upright piano, creating a warm, Victorian atmosphere. In just a few weeks, the newly hired pianist and his ragtime melodies were packing the club every night. The Maple Leaf's pianist had a musical charm that listeners could not resist.

During quiet afternoons when there were no customers about, Scott sat at the Maple Leaf piano and began to get his music down on paper. By summer, he had two compositions that he felt were ready for sale. The first he named "Original Rags." The other he named "Maple Leaf Rag." Scott took them to A.W. Perry and Son, a Sedalia publisher. Perry looked over the handwritten sheets while the composer stood waiting.

After a few moments, he handed the music back. "I'm sorry," he said. "This music just does not meet our needs."

Scott was disappointed, of course, but not defeated. "I'm going to take them to Kansas City," he told Otis.

In Kansas City, publisher Carl Hoffman carefully looked over the two pieces of music. "I'll take a chance on 'Original Rags,'" he told the waiting composer. Scott was excited. At last he would see his work published.

"Hoffman took 'Original Rags'!" Scott told Otis on his return to Sedalia.

Saunders was delighted. "You've done it, Joplin," he cried. "You've sold your first piece of music!"

Joplin had mixed feelings about his trip to Kansas City. He was happy that he'd been able to sell "Original Rags," but he had thought "Maple Leaf Rag" would sell as well. As the composer, he knew it was the better of the two rags. The listeners who gathered around his piano at night must have thought so, too, because they requested it often. It was becoming Scott's unofficial theme song.

In spite of his disappointment, Scott went on playing "Maple Leaf" at the club and worked on new compositions as well. By summer of 1899, he had created "Sunflower Slow Drag," and he still had his heart set on getting "Maple Leaf Rag" published. There was a music-store owner in town who had recently begun a publishing business. Scott decided to give him a try.

On a hot August afternoon, he walked into John Stark's store, "Sunflower Slow Drag" and "Maple Leaf Rag" in hand. John Stark had often dropped by the club and was a fan of Scott's. He was interested in seeing what Scott had to show him. Perhaps there was a business opportunity in it, he thought. However, when he saw the manuscript, the veteran music-store owner shook his head.

"The problem with your rags, Joplin, is that they are *too* good," Stark said. "The average sheet music buyer would never be skilled enough to play them."

Stark's son William did not quite agree with his father. "Maybe they won't be able to play them, but they might like to try. Play the rags for us," he said to Scott. So Scott sat down at the music-store piano and played. John Stark stood by the window, listening. As Scott began to play, a small boy standing just outside the store window began to dance. The young dancer's feet fairly flew to the beat of Joplin's music.

John Stark had to agree with his son. There was something special about this Joplin music—it was so *danceable!* The senior Mr. Stark went to his desk and drew up a contract for "Maple Leaf Rag."

Scott Joplin's own favorite rag had finally found a home. No doubt the composer himself fairly danced out of the music store that August afternoon.

Copies of "Maple Leaf Rag" were very popular with Sedalian music lovers. Difficult or not, it seemed that the fans of the popular piano player wanted to tackle his music for themselves. The problem for John Stark & Son was that there just were not enough musicians in Sedalia. It took an entire year to sell 400 copies. Still, this Joplin music held real promise. The only other music the Starks were publishing had been composed by their friends and relatives. Scott Joplin's music seemed to be the key to the future success of their new business. The Starks decided to expand their publishing operation and take it to a larger music market—St. Louis.

Better promotion, the invention of automatic player pianos, and the rising popularity of the new record player known as the gramophone all worked in favor of the new publishing company. An expanded listening audience was anxious to try to play the music of the rising young composer.

In just a few months, 50,000 copies of "Maple Leaf Rag" had been sold.

The Starks wanted Scott to follow them to St. Louis, but Scott held back. There was a new interest in his life now; her name was Belle Hayden. Scott knew that Belle loved him. But did she love him enough to leave her friends and family for the sake of his music? Scott wasn't certain.

## Chapter Four

Ragtime was becoming more and more popular. Competitions known as "cutting contests" were now a favorite form of entertainment—both with the performers themselves and with the public. Rag players would come to the Maple Leaf Club from all over the country to challenge one another. Each player brought his own rooting section of fans, for the player receiving the most cheers would be declared the winner. The greatest challenge of all was Scott Joplin, and Sedalians turned out in great numbers to support their hometown player. They cheered so loudly that it was a rare night when Scott Joplin did not win. He was becoming known as the "King of Ragtime."

Joplin's reputation was growing, and he realized that there would be even more opportunity to advance his career in St. Louis. So in the summer of 1901, he and Belle moved to St. Louis to start a new life. Scott Joplin was a happy man. He loved Belle, his reputation as a composer was growing, and, almost best of all, parents were bringing their children to him for piano lessons. Teaching was rewarding to Scott, and it suited his quiet personality.

Belle, though, was not happy. She loved Scott, but she had little feeling for the music that was the center of his life. The constant piano playing and stream of students in and out of her home annoyed her. Scott thought Belle might come to appreciate music if she could take part in it, so he began giving her violin lessons. Belle's progress was slow. She just did not have the desire to play the instrument.

Scott's new life in St. Louis was busy, but he kept on composing. John Stark published more and more Joplin numbers. He quickly added

"Swipesy Cakewalk" after "Maple Leaf Rag" to keep the Joplin name prominent. Then he added Joplin's "Sunflower Slow Drag," "Augustan Club Waltz," and "Peacherine Rag" to his list. The cover of "Peacherine" read, "By the King of Ragtime Writers, Scott Joplin." Scott's reputation as top in his field was nationwide now.

In 1902, John Stark published Joplin's "The Entertainer." It would become the composer's most successful piece of music. In 1903, two more pieces, "The Favorite" and "The Sycamore," were published by Stark.

Meanwhile, Belle had become increasingly unhappy. She and Scott were always at odds. However, Belle was expecting a baby, and Scott hoped that the joy of their first child would lift Belle's spirits. A little girl was born to them early in 1903. Scott's dream for happiness at home was not to be realized, though. The baby was not healthy and lived for only a few months.

Scott began to find it difficult to compose. In addition to his personal sadness, he began to have disagreements with his publisher. Joplin wanted to publish a ragtime ballet, and he had ideas about writing a ragtime opera. Stark felt ragtime would not sell in these forms and refused to take an interest in Scott's new ideas.

Ragtime was changing. Publishers were now turning out "New York Style" ragtime. The old African rhythms that Scott had built his compositions on were not apparent in this new, fast-paced music. Scott Joplin had strong feelings about ragtime keeping its original form. He stopped going to the playing contests at the Rosebud Café in St. Louis, for the contests had become no more than tests of how fast a pianist could play.

Scott and Belle could not seem to find happiness together, and finally they parted. Performing, composing, and his personal life no longer held any joy for Scott Joplin, and he felt very much alone. He wanted to see his family again. He decided to go to Texarkana.

The unhappy composer must have been turning over many questions in his mind during the train ride back to his boyhood town. He had seen his brothers Will and Robert off and on through the years. But what about Monroe? And his sisters? What had become of them? Mama and Papa were getting old now. Would he find them all right? It had been nine years since he had had any contact with home. Little by little, the Joplin family had drifted apart.

At last the train pulled into Texarkana's small station. The town had changed very little. Chickens scratched about in front yards as always. A tangle of boys played tag in the dusty street, just as Scott and his brothers had done. It all seemed so long ago. Scott walked up one street and down another until he reached Mount Zion Church. He stopped and stared. The church *had* changed. A proud new church building stood in place of the old house in which Scott had attended Sunday meetings. He went inside hoping to find Florence Joplin at work.

There was no one about but a man polishing the pews. Must be the caretaker, Scott thought. Caretaker? But where was Mama? That was her job.

"Miss Florence passed on a few years back," the new caretaker informed his visitor. "My, how she did love to ring the new church bell," he remembered out loud. "Rang it for every meeting, and whenever somebody died."

Scott was filled with sadness. How often had she stood ringing the church bell, wondering if she would see her music-loving son again? Who had tolled the bell for Mama? "Are there any Joplins left in town?" he asked.

"Mr. Monroe Joplin and his family live over at 815 Ash Street, and old Mr. Joplin, too," the man said.

Scott hurried over to Ash Street. He knocked on the door of a house much like the one he had grown up in. The surprised Joplins quickly drew him inside. Papa walked with a stick now, Scott saw. The years of hard railroad labor had weakened his legs. "A little bit of leg trouble," Papa said. "It's nothing." What were a few aches compared to seeing his long-gone son?

"Sit down, sit down. Rosa has supper about ready," Monroe urged. His wife set an extra place at the table, and they all began asking each other question after question. There was so much to catch up on.

"Where are Osie and Myrtle?" Scott wanted to know. Both had married and moved farther into Arkansas, he learned. "You should hear those girls sing," Papa said proudly. "Reminds me of the old days." Osie and Myrtle both worked as cooks, but the Joplin love of music had never left them.

"Play something for us," Monroe urged when the dishes had been cleared away. Scott sat down at the piano and began to play.

"Where did you find such wonderful music?" Monroe asked. Scott sat back on the piano bench and looked around at his family. "It's my own," he said.

Fred, Donita, Ethel, and Mattie, Scott's nephew and nieces, had already been put to bed. It soon became clear that they were not sleeping, though. Four pairs of feet quickly descended the stairs. "Do you mean that you are a composer, Uncle Scott?" Mattie asked. Mattie was taking piano lessons and knew enough about music to be in awe of a composer.

"Are you famous, Uncle Scott?" Fred wanted to know.

Scott Joplin smiled at the idea. "Well, not yet," he said. He went on playing. Rosa let the children stay up past midnight. This was an event they would long remember.

The next day, Scott went down to the town music store. He was quickly invited to play the piano. Listeners gathered in small groups. A big-city composer in town was news. Their admiration lifted Scott's spirits and encouraged him to pay a visit to his old music teacher, J.C. Johnson. As a teacher himself now, Scott realized how much those early lessons with Mr. Johnson and his elementary school teacher had influenced his life.

Scott was enjoying his visit home; seeing much of his family again had refreshed his spirits. He knew, though, that it was time to go back to St. Louis. Scott felt ready to compose again, and he was sure he could do it now.

Back in St. Louis, he sat down at the piano with a pen and some sheets of blank manuscript paper at hand. Much to his alarm, the music still would not come. He began to feel that he had lost his touch forever.

What could be done? Friends advised a change of scene, something really different. Scott Joplin became a wanderer again.

# Chapter Five

By 1907, Scott Joplin had made his way to New York City. The fast-paced life in this center of the nation's music-publishing business was uplifting. The composer found that he *could* write again. The bright titles of his works, named for flowers, reflect his renewed hope—"Gladiolus Rag," "Rose Leaf Rag," and "Heliotrope Bouquet."

While visiting Washington, D.C., Scott had met and married Lottie Stokes. Lottie was enthusiastic about her husband's work and turned their New York City home into a boarding house for young musicians. The added income from the boarders gave Scott the security to go on with his work, and the talk of music that went around Lottie's supper table sparked Scott's creativity. Another stream of Joplin rags went to press—"Pine Apple Rag," "Sugar Cane Rag," "Fig Leaf Rag." Life had become sweet again for Scott Joplin.

In 1908, Scott went to work on a project that was dear to his heart—a ragtime opera. *Treemonisha* was set on a ficticious southwestern plantation during the 1880s. Ned and Monisha, a black couple who badly want a child, find a baby under a tree. They name her Monisha after her mother, but the child soon becomes known by the pet name, Tree-Monisha. Treemonisha grows up to be a leader in the black community. By educating her followers, she persuades them to forsake the witchcraft and other forms of ignorance that are hindering their lives. The plot was a simple one, but Scott Joplin had a definite purpose in mind— to show that black Americans, with strength, education, and perseverance, could overcome the sad effects of slavery.

Scott felt so strongly about delivering the message of his opera that he drove himself to compose not only the music itself, but the story, orchestra parts, and dances as well. It took him two years to finish the project. To Joplin's disappointment, John Stark refused to publish the work. He did not think a ragtime opera would pay back its publishing expenses. Next, Scott tried the New York publishers, but one after another they gave him the same answer—"A ragtime opera won't sell."

Scott was not about to give up. He decided to publish the opera himself. Self-publishing was risky, and the Joplins did not have much money to work with. Neither did most of their friends. Another year went by before the opera was printed, and then came the problem of finding a theater that would produce it. After two years of searching, Scott was finally able to convince the manager of the Lafayette Theatre in Harlem to take on the opera. The men discussed the opera, and the manager set a performance date of fall 1913.

Scott looked at the man in amazement. "This fall!" he said. "But it is *August* now. Do you mean to say that I must find singers, dancers, and an orchestra—not to mention rehearse the opera—all within a month?"

"Take it or leave it," the manager said. Scott took it. He quickly placed an advertisement for performers in the New York papers.

Fall arrived, but *Treemonisha* was not performed. The theater had suddenly come under new management. "Our customers want comedy," the new managers told Scott, "not drama." Scott Joplin was in despair. This opera meant so much to him. In 1915, he rented another theater, gathered his singers and dancers, and played the orchestra parts himself on the piano. Joplin was determined to see *Treemonisha* performed.

The well-written opera was full of winning songs. The dances were fascinating. Sadly, however, the performance was not a success. There were problems over which Scott Joplin had no control. For one thing, the theater was in Harlem, a black neighborhood. White operagoers were hesitant to attend a Harlem performance by an all-black cast. Black operagoers were not interested, either. They had come to New York to begin a new way of life, and glamour and style were what they wanted for entertainment. A story about slavery was the last thing they wanted to see. It was a very small audience that greeted Scott Joplin's dream project.

As if the failure of his opera were not enough, Joplin also had to face the sad truth that ragtime was reaching the end of its popularity. America was entering the age of jazz. While ragtime made its contribution to this new free-form style of music, players and listeners were no longer satisfied with the slow, steady pulse of the rag.

Selling ragtime music, no matter how good it was, was becoming more and more difficult.

With the failure of his opera, Scott's dream of elevating ragtime to the level of classical music was destroyed. What depressed Scott even more, though, was that he felt he had failed to deliver his opera's message. By 1916, Scott Joplin was a broken man. His spirit was gone, and disease was taking over his body. On April 1, 1917, the day the United States entered World War I, Scott Joplin died. He was buried in an unmarked grave on New York's Long Island. The ceremony for the soft-spoken, 49-year-old musician was a simple one, attended only by Lottie and a few New York acquaintances.

"Play 'Maple Leaf Rag' at my funeral," Scott Joplin had said to Lottie before he died. Lottie did not have the piece played. She felt that it would be inappropriate. In later years, the composer's widow often shook her head and said, "How I have regretted that decision."

There may have been no ragtime music played at the unmarked grave in New York that day, but "Maple Leaf Rag" and many other Joplin compositions still sing in the hearts of those who love ragtime music.

# AFTERWORD

Scott Joplin was a man ahead of his time. In 1972, the Atlanta Arts Center performed *Treemonisha*. Three years later, the Houston Grand Opera presented the performance with rave reviews, and, that same year, *Treemonisha* opened on Broadway. Joplin's "The Entertainer" set off a new ragtime craze when it was selected as the theme song for the award-winning movie *The Sting*.

Ragtime festivals are held all over the United States now. Players, dressed in everything from Gay Nineties to Roaring Twenties garb, engage in cutting contests like those young Scott Joplin so enjoyed. The contests are judged by ragtime enthusiasts, just as in the old days. Players are required to demonstrate their skills in both the later, faster ragtime style and in the classic style of the Joplin period. Each contestant must play "Maple Leaf Rag." Scott Joplin's own favorite has become a standard for judging ragtime skill.